Seeing
In a Small Town

poems by

Pasquale Trozzolo

Finishing Line Press
Georgetown, Kentucky

Seeing
In a Small Town

To passersby, in small towns and large.

And to librarians, Dollar Store employees, Greyhound Bus riders, cowboys who flirt at the Billy Goat Tavern, and all those who meet up at Casey's.

Copyright © 2024 by Pasquale Trozzolo
ISBN 979-8-88838-821-1 First Edition
All rights reserved under International and Pan-American Copyright Conventions. No part of this book may be reproduced in any manner whatsoever without written permission from the publisher, except in the case of brief quotations embodied in critical articles and reviews.

ACKNOWLEDGMENTS

The author is grateful to the editors of the following journals in which poems of this book previously appeared, sometimes in a slightly different form or with another title:

50 Give or Take—Vine Leaves Press: Flirting at the Corner Bar
Last Leaves Magazine: Quiet at the Library
105 Meadowlark Reader: Small Victory on Hickory Street
Molecule Lit Mag: Tornado Warning in Daviess County
Syncopation Literary Journal: Fading Music at the County Fair
The Ravens Perch: Bird Watching by the River
Tiny Seed Literary Journal: Sitting Under an Oak Tree
What Rough Beast: Pizza at Casey's

Publisher: Leah Huete de Maines
Editor: Christen Kincaid
Cover Art: Mark English
Author Photo: Mark Versluis
Cover Design: Elizabeth Maines McCleavy

Order online: www.finishinglinepress.com
also available on amazon.com

Author inquiries and mail orders:
Finishing Line Press
PO Box 1626
Georgetown, Kentucky 40324
USA

Contents

Fly Over 1

Forewarned 2

He Lives in an Airbnb 3

Quiet at the Library 4

Checkout at the Dollar Store 5

The Couple in the Middle Booth Become One 6

Smile on the Greyhound 7

Pizza at Casey's 8

Overheard at Billy Goat Tavern 9

Fading Music at the County Fair 10

Bird Watching by the River 11

Opposing Booths at the Diner 12

Leaving the Travelodge 13

Flirting at the Corner Bar 14

Waiting at Cameron Regional Medical Center 15

Fishing at First Light 16

The Old Couple Down the Road 17

Missing at Creekmore Cemetery 18

He Visits Her on Sundays 19

Small Victory on Hickory Street 20

Shopping in Jamesport 21

Mannequin at Elbert's Department Store 22

It's No Picnic at Beach #2 23

Sitting Under an Oak Tree 24

Envy at the Window 26

Tornado Warning in Daviess County 27

Rocking on the Front Porch 28

Old Winds Blow on the Prairie 29

*...and we drink our coffee and pretend
not to look at each other.*
—*Charles Bukowski*

Fly Over

You know that game where you see a person, couple, or group and begin to make a story around them? It's a great way to meet spies, murderers, vagabonds, lovers, and thieves. The running dialogue of this game is best imagined with your date or significant other. What you learn about your accomplice is always surprising as the plot thickens.

Of course, you can also play this game as a single storyteller. The only requirement is to see someone or something and imagine what is or is not. Now, caution is advised. Too long a stare, and you might find yourself on the receiving end of punch. Playing this game too often alone in the same place might result in a restraining order!

This book of poems grew from real and imagined observations collected in small towns. Passing through, there is much to miss in small-town America. And even when we do see, we often make assumptions based on our predisposed expectations, quickly judging each person by their cover and not allowing the story to develop. And, just like books, it's almost always a mistake—we are always playing the story game, it turns out.

What do we miss when we judge based on an earring, tattoo, cigarette, skin color, rusty pickup truck, or a shade of lipstick? All people and most places carry their burdens, strengths, sufferings, broken hearts, and love stories. Even in a small town—perhaps especially in a small town. And, when you let your imagination create the storyline, poems sometimes appear.

The poems found in *Seeing—In a Small Town* offer just one view, looking slightly below and inside the daily routines through the eyes of a passerby. Each vignette is written hoping the reader recognizes that we should judge slowly and carefully—if at all.

Forewarned

What I write and
what you read
are not always
the same.
For example—
sometimes
you're right.

He Lives in an Airbnb

Alone I sit in a bar full of strangers on a well-worn stool—the old guy with a notebook sipping a gin and tonic. Fitting in has never been my strong suit. Now, I wonder what the mid-40s couple shooting pool might think about me—if they were to play the story game.

Tonight
he seems borrowed—
rented.
He is loitering
in someone else's place—
pretending
he's not wrong.

Quiet at the Library

The Daviess County Library is my playground for the afternoon as I search for a quiet place to read, write, and generally waste time. I'm failing at the writing part and begin to look around and soon a story finds me, this time with red hair and what I imagine must be a long career as a librarian.

Soft sounds abound
but for the encroachment of
keys clicking a small distraction of reality.
Amid this low racket, she reads—slow—absorbing the
shape of each word—carefully turning pages as if separating the
ink to claim her story. Casually she moves hair, tucking messy
strands behind perfect ears—and pushes glasses against
the slope of her nose, killing me from a distance.
Like Shakespeare, I wish to be a glove—that I might.
She closes her eyes—seeing—what she reads. And me,
knowing she's here only for the books, I write her,
wondering what journey she's on and how I might,
in this quiet, find her again tomorrow.

Checkout at the Dollar Store

Dollar stores. They're everywhere, and on this Saturday morning, I find myself at the DG on Highway 6. As I wait in line, I notice the checker is greeting everyone by name. At first, she appears a little scary with her bright red T-shirt and arms full of tattoos—a pack of Salems and pink Bic within easy reach. Yet, as the line moves, I hear her sweet conversations with each customer, and I fall under a spell.

Like thrift store shoes she has a history—
well-aged, untold—a slightly uneven wear.
Her beauty-parlor blonde streaks a graying
invitation to discover what whispers through her years.
Secrets await my desire to embrace everything about her.
I want to feel her tense, know her past—tug her truth through
miles of gravel clouds knowing it's not too late to answer
the warmth of her greeting. The soft pink tint of fading ink peeking
from her right shoulder holds my gaze urging a search for more skin,
wondering where her signs might lead. My items now checked,
it's time to pay and leave behind this resplendent mystery.

The Couple in the Middle Booth Become One

Even from across the room it's easy to see this is not the first rodeo for this couple. They are well practiced, precise even. Still, they seem nice. I hope I'm wrong.

She thinks—
he'll be back—

like all the other times.

He thinks—
she'll never change—

like all the other times.

Sadly—
they're both right.

Smile on the Greyhound

The bus trip to the town proclaiming itself the birthplace of J.C. Penny and now the Quilt Capital of America (which also has a pretty good little brewery) is relatively smooth. Buses are grand for people-watching and story-making, so I watch as a young man shyly smiles at a young woman, slightly out of his league. Hope springs eternal, and some memories last a lifetime, even when made in just seconds

Two rows up
close enough for fragrance to float

she smiles at him
with an East Coast look

he knows he will
never see her again yet always remember

that face
on bus number three sixty-one.

Pizza at Casey's

Casey's is famous for gas, pizza, and running into old friends. As I fill the tank, I watch a man and a woman greet each other. It's obvious that they were once close and they're catching up on the fly. There is even a slight hug and quick kiss on the cheek. But what if?

What if we met in a bar
What if we drank bourbon
What if it was 10:00 p.m.
What if there was a dark corner?

What if we met on a train
What if I asked what you're reading
What if you read poems
What if I knew all the lines?

What if we met in a gallery
What if we loved the same art
What if you asked me to hold your hand
What if we didn't stop there?

What if I saw your red dress
What if we met on the dance floor
What if I knew how to tango
What if you liked my embrace?

Overheard at Billy Goat Tavern

I love this place. It's dark enough, and both old and young fit in. It's almost closing time, and the couple across from me is conversing emotionally. I don't want to eavesdrop, but I do manage to catch a few words, enough to, you know.

Make up. She says she wants
to make up.

He seems glad for her touching lies—
sometimes that's all we need.

Without thinking,
he wants to go again—

Get twisted—predictable
as old shoelaces. Forever tangled.

He knows—she's still married—
the air still dirty.

She touches him. All
hell breaks loose. They sin everywhere

Fading Music at the County Fair

This county has a fair. There are rides for the kids, lots of flags, goats, pigs, and a band. The music catches me. I'm standing blocks from the bandstand, yet I hear the distant song. The notes carry me back to a teenage summer with my first love. We spent so much time together that we could practically wear each other's tans. I can still smell the lemons in her shampoo and feel her silken hair falling onto my face. Today the distant music brings tears to my eyes and pencil to my notebook.

Listening—I hear loud music playing softly
with distant whispers, repeating lyrics—
murmurs of long exhausted love still beating.
Like a shaken tambourine the rattle is slightly off-key,
background for someone else's song. Notes play lonely
sounds as words escape in layers, stirring long-dormant desires.
Barely audible they harmonize—perfect memories reminding me
of lyrics we once sang. Sounds float, lifting my spirits out of
range, remembering our love and hoping you sometimes
hear loud music playing softly.

Bird Watching by the River

As I walk along the Grand River on this cool spring morning, I am delighted that no one is around to prompt a story or other tall tale—but there is a hawk.

Does the hawk mind flying alone
wondering if they will wait at the nest
or fly on without him? Even as he flies
he cries, silently so as to fool.
His wings pull him,
clouds his only company.
He's higher now but not less worried.
Just more practiced.

Opposing Booths at the Diner

Blue-plate specials are still a thing in some places. I wait for my meatloaf and try to pay attention to Phil, my lunch companion, as he talks about wood and how to make good cuts. But I'm distracted by movement over Phil's right shoulder. It's just a slight head nod and quick eye contact. Story games are back.

We sit six feet apart.
In this heat, our eyes meet.
It would be nice to find you
without the company—with the heat.
And the indulgence of a full menu.

Leaving the Travelodge

Parking lots attract long and animated conversations, especially motel parking lots. I can't help but notice the Audi RS parked outside room 8, with a well-dressed couple having a lively discussion. She looks happy. Him, not so much. Poor guy.

I'm just here for fun, she answers
before he even finishes the question.
Softly she blows smoke his way then kisses him
hard. He wants to complain, but she warned him,
said she would love him like a nomad—
now, watching her come and go is
meaningless at best.

Flirting at the Corner Bar

Bars are a main draw on Main Street. Each is filled with the predictable and the unforeseen. For example, just a few stools down, a sophisticated lady seems to enjoy the banter with a hopeful young cowboy.

"Make it a double," she said.
Immediately drawn, he moved three stools down.
That was his first mistake.
"I'll have what she's having"—
his second mistake.
Then the big one, looking into those tumultuous eyes.
Ten minutes of small talk, and he was in love—
until her wife showed up.

Waiting at Cameron Regional Medical Center

This hook is deep, a fishhook that is, and today it brings me to Cameron Regional. Here I wait along with a very pensive-looking couple in the next row. Does anyone like waiting—for anything? The worst is waiting here, at a hospital. Yet we all get here eventually. We wait with fear rising as time passes. Hopelessly realizing that, for some things, we are indeed helpless. The man in the next row holds a rosary, which may add hope but also fear.

Is there anything quite as
Agonizing as the wait
That long useless time
Moving not at all?

Waiting for
Is worst of all
So slowly
Nothing.

Then the time
Does truly come
Past is present
Facts become.

Is it serious
Can she be fixed
How long will we
Be waiting?

Fishing at First Light

Fishing can be peaceful and sometimes enlightening. Sounds travel far on the lake, especially in the hush of daybreak. Deep down Three Tubes Cove, I hear brushing sounds with a slow but familiar beat.

Sun barely up I hear him—
earlier today than yesterday,
scraping the wood with his methodical push—
drearily sweeping a creaking porch with a broom
he struggles to hold, bristling with a past now left in pieces.
He bends dangerously low, collecting what he can in a
dustpan as old as he and pauses, meditating like an
ancient monk, finding something vital that he
has seen before. I watch him thinking as
he ponders his dust and what awaits.

The Old Couple Down the Road

Just around the bend is a lovely old lake house. I see a U-Haul in the drive and several folks this morning. The older man stands on the porch, drinks coffee, and looks upward as if searching.

She predicted it.
Said he should get with
the program. Sell all the old stock.
He never thought it would come so fast.
Should have been more time to get ready.
Now she's all business. In a sudden hurry.
Clearing shelves, emptying closets. Accelerating.
She can still pack. Like there's no tomorrow.
Today they move. Carrying a heavy heritage.
To their dependent home. Forgetting the future.

Missing at Creekmore Cemetery

Today I visit Creekmore Cemetery hoping to find some of the James Gang. Instead, I see a man praying. Loss needs no explanation, no rescue. Loss is just loss—and hurt.

Is that her
Fragrance
In the air.

Is that her
Dress
And her hair.

Is that her
Breath
On my face.

Is that her
Glance
And her lace.

Is that her
Whisper.

Is that her
Touch.

Is that her
Heart
Still beating.

He Visits Her on Sundays

Just about every small town has a town square. That's where you'll find the bank, diner, bar, hardware store, and all of life's necessities. Park benches attract sitters, and trees attract birds. This Sunday afternoon, my subject is the woman in a green sundress conversing with a cardinal.

Red lands,
here I am, he seems to speak,
and that hair—has he gone punk in his new world?
As if to answer, Red flutters one branch over and stares.
Many people believe this is how they visit us. Dressed in red, with
batman eyes and wings. She's always thought it was just a pretty bird.
Now, watching him stare at her, not moving, pointing with his bill,
she's not so sure anymore. Perhaps she should test him.
Red flutters again, moves one branch over, back turned toward her.
Well, I guess he doesn't like that idea—
more of the blind faith type, love doesn't die, and all that.
Red flies to the bench, wings flapping, touches her hand
gently with his beak, and stares. Yes, it's him—
always able to prove a point.
Even now.

Small Victory on Hickory Street

In unusual places, we sometimes find our true selves—or what we hope to be true. And so, as I walk along Hickory Street, a squirrel helps define me.

I saw a squirrel today darting,
stopping, and darting again. Undecided or
careful? Certain or confused? Hunting or hunted?
Quick stop. Full run. Which direction will he go? Then
I saw the car. And the squirrel saw it too. We froze. Move
squirrel, move! Closer, closer, and closer. Move, for God's sake,
move. He just stared, clear-eyed. No wasted movements. My
little squirrel standing resolute against a shiny Chevy. And then,
with only inches to spare he darted away.
Safe. Proud. Victorious. And yes—
I now feed him every day.

Shopping in Jamesport

The Farm House Collection Shop in Jamesport is the place for hand and body lotions, soaps of all kinds, unusual candies, and special spices. But it's the candles that draw a crowd. Today, the makers are crafting various sizes of wild currant and sandalwood. Watching along with the crowd is a father and his three young daughters. There were smiles and even a little laughter, but the fragrance was too much for him.

Upon a certain occurrence, I think of you.

like hearing the word whisper—
or seeing blue in their eyes,
or the faintest fragrance of sandalwood,
or when light is low or bright,
or the shower glass is covered in steam,
or a dog barks, or it's time for church or walking,
or the taste of butterscotch, or scotch scotch,
or when clearing snow or starting the car,
or birthdays, or wind, or bedtime stories,
or the sound of pages turning,
or when it's time to brush their teeth,
or the times they miss you most.

Mannequin at Elbert's Department Store

Elbert's Department Store is a fascinating place. Here it doesn't matter if you're big or tall or small or short. They have everything, including a mannequin in the window. This mannequin is a friend of mine, and every time I pass it, I give it a look. Each time I see something new, but the voice is always the same—

Why do you change me?
I like the way I am.
You always push me,
Making me try what's new,
To see if they will like me
When all that matters is you.
I don't like it,
Everyone rushing by.
Even when you're dressing me,
They never look inside.
Hide me in the storeroom
Let me take my rest.
No change for me, please
Let me be myself.

It's No Picnic at Beach #2

Beautiful Lake Viking offers great spots for a picnic, including the creatively named Beach #2. It is here that I see a couple sitting quietly on a blanket, watching a single-engine plane pass overhead.

Impending—
Up and then off
they echo and stall.
It feels like they might
come to an abrupt end.
These stunts of theirs
scrape the sky with
terror and hope
vibrating through
their own shadows.
A distant but familiar
pulse beckons.
Will they throttle up or
is this the end?

Sitting Under an Oak Tree

Fall is my favorite writing season. There seem to be people of interest everywhere. This afternoon my pen falls on a man wearing a fishing vest, sitting on the ground, gear nearby, and profoundly concentrating on a leaf as it flies past him.

You know the sound—
That light scrape of leaf
Once fallen.

Like an old transistor
Radio switched on
It crackles

Passing along the street
With grace and a
Gentle disturbance.

Traveling lightly, it
Changes direction
So easily.

Does it know its destination?
Does it know it's
Already dead?

Yet still it travels
And crackles and
Finds him.

He wants to follow
But is catching
Only fragments.

Does this fallen leaf
Now out of sight know he
Misses her?

He remembers how she moved
Sharp, crisp.
And stirring.

And that crackle—
He cries
To hear it again.

Envy at the Window

Peacefully drinking coffee one early spring morning at Country Roads Cafe, I hear a bang and then another even louder. The source remains a mystery for a few more hits, and then I see it. A robin flying wildly into the cafe window. What's all this, I wonder? A suicide pact among the birds? Turns out it's berries, reflections, short memoirs, and such. And envy.

There is a window by the
door with a tree close by. Its
spring berries attract attention of
the birds especially. They land—they
feast. Under the influence, they fly only
to crash into the window. Some die, most
recover. To land. To feast. To fly, under the
influence all over again. What do these birds know?
How can they so soon forget and fly without regret to
so easily crash again? I want to know.

Tornado Warning in Daviess County

Severe weather in tornado alley—there is nothing like it. Perhaps it's the buildup. Most of the time, we know it's coming hours, sometimes days ahead. But still, when it arrives, it's full of surprises.

Soft lightning.
Distant. Quiet. Quick.
Yet the air is charged.
Danger on the horizon.
A good night to write.
I haven't killed anyone
yet, but I'm still holding my
pencil, and there are pages.
If I were you, I would move
slowly away from the window.

Rocking on the Front Porch

My travels to small towns and large are so much more exciting with my wife by my side. She always adds to the story and still likes to rock.

Young days now
gone yet still we play.
Our buffet offers deeper choices.
With fewer blind spots, I see all of you.
Dressed only in the morning light
your moves abduct me.
In no special hurry our
desire slowly ages.
We travel, taking forever.

Old Winds Blow on the Prairie

Time to head back to the city. I'll be back to feel these winds and whimsy, God willing.

Winds blow Kansas dust
        like words—they swirl

into thoughts and drift—
        disappearing only to

reappear with more meaning—
        or less grit

of dreams, floating to clouds
        later falling to smudge my future pages

waiting
        not to forget that this

State was once home to
        many who are not here.

With Thanks

Thank you to poets and authors Catherine Abbey Hodges and Marcela Sulak, whose review, suggestions, and thoughtfulness provided the right push to complete this collection. Thank you to Lisa Phillips for crossing t's and dotted i's. And, as always, thanks to my wife Joan for her support, faith, and love. There is no poetry without you.

Thank you to the people in small towns throughout Northwest Missouri and eastern Kansas for ignoring my stares and my notebook. These poems are part fact, part fiction, and substantially influenced by an aging imagination, summer afternoons spent on the town square in Gallatin, Missouri, and too much time at Dollar General. This is a work of fiction and is not intended to portray any person or combination of persons living or dead—unless it does.

About the Cover: The Farmer by Mark English

Mr. English (September 19, 1933 – August 8, 2019) was an American illustrator and painter born in Hubbard, Texas. He was a leading illustrator for major publications in a career spanning from the 1960s to the 1990s before beginning a career painting for gallery exhibition in 1995. His unique illustration style appeared in publications such as *Time Magazine, Sports Illustrated, Redbook, Atlantic Monthly, Rolling Stone, TV Guide, McCall*'s, and many others. He designed 14 U.S. postage stamps and album covers for John Denver, Julian Lennon, and The Who. He is one of the most awarded illustrators in the history of the Society of Illustrators. The author wishes to express a special thank you to Wendy English and the English families for permission to use this work.

Pasquale Trozzolo is a retired madman from Kansas. His work appears in numerous journals and anthologies, including *Sunspot Literary Journal, The Pangolin Review, What Rough Beast, 34th Parallel, From Whispers to Roar*s, and *50 Give or Take.* He is the author of two chapbooks, *Before the Distance* (The Poetry Box, December 2020) and *UN/Reconciled* (Kelsay Books, October 2022). Still no tattoos, or MFA, he continues to complicate his life by living out as many retirement clichés as possible, including acting like 70 is the new 50.

https://pasqualetrozzolo.com
@poetpasquale
#ptrozzolo

Milton Keynes UK
Ingram Content Group UK Ltd.
UKHW031206251124
451566UK00005B/40